FABULOUS FRITTON LAKE

The story of Walter Mussett,
Norfolk gamekeeper extraordinary,
and his love for one of East Anglia's
greatest beauty spots.

Keith Skipper

TAGMAN

First published in Great Britain in the year 2003 by
The Tagman Press, an imprint of Tagman Worldwide Ltd

The Tagman Press
Lovemore House, PO Box 754, Norwich,
Norfolk NR1 4GY, UK
and 1888 Century Park East, Suite 1900,
Los Angeles CA 90067-1702, USA

www.tagman-press.com
email: editorial@tagman-press.com

ISBN: 1-903571-14-6

A CIP catalogue record for this book is available from
The British Library

Set in Caslon Open Face and Granjon
Designed by Dick Malt
Edited by Bridget Bagshaw and Caroline Merz
Main cover photographs by Anthony Grey
Printed by Franklyn, Macclesfield, Cheshire SK10 1LL

TAGMAN

L639.95

CONTENTS

Lord and Lady Somerleyton

Everyone who has ever met Walter Mussett finds at once that he has a natural charm, an enormous capacity for hard work and enthusiasm for whatever challenge comes his way. All this is combined with a wonderful sense of humour.

A statue stands on the lawn at Fritton, sculpted by Kathleen Scott, the mother of Sir Peter Scott, in memory of five of his boyhood friends who were killed in the war. Two of them, Tom and Julius Jackson, lived at Herringfleet Hall. When I look at the statue I have happy memories of the Jackson boys and Walter going ratting, with me occasionally being allowed along too, being eight years younger than them!

You will read in this book of Walter's childhood, which was not always easy, his war service in the Middle East, his life as a keeper at Somerleyton and Morningthorpe and then, until retirement, as manager of Fritton Lake Country Park. He was successful in all these enterprises, perhaps because he always gives that little bit extra.

Walter and his wife Peggy are a first class team. Together, they made the Fritton Lake Country Park a great success story for the Somerleyton Estate. Under their guidance it progressed beyond all our expectations. I am delighted, therefore, to write this foreword and commend this book to anyone who has the countryside at heart.

'… the wooded borders of the lake had lost none of their charm.'

My father, Alfred Grey, fishing at Fritton

Publishing this combined biography of a man and a lake in the year 2003 through The Tagman Press completes a story that for me goes back more than fifty years. It's a love story in essence because, without realising it then, I fell in love at first sight with Fritton Lake in 1952 at the age of 14. Another 30 years would pass before I met Walter Mussett, the remarkable former gamekeeper who helped Lord Somerleyton transform the lake into a modern country park without spoiling its timeless charm. But the seeds of the story were sown in the year Queen Elizabeth II was crowned.

I was a city boy, born in Norwich, and a family friend brought me to fish from a boat on the lake that year. We arrived at the deserted Haddiscoe station by train early in the morning and took a local taxi to the lake, arriving along a narrow lane where the hedges brushed both sides of the car. A Mr Ward farmed the land around the lake in those days. I remember him as a friendly figure of soldierly bearing and he conducted us personally to the boat sheds through the formal walled gardens, where, if I remember rightly, a few exotic birds with brightly coloured plumage squawked echoingly in their cages.

There were no other fishermen about that morning and it probably happened whilst we were rowing southward to fish in one of the quieter bays close to the far shore – falling in love with the lake, that is. All that could be seen from the boat was the blue sky, the wonderful unbroken green fringes of trees and reeds and the glittering silver surface of the water.

Fritton Lake.

FRITTON LAKE

Crested grebe and moorhens dived and popped up all around the boat, a pleasant breeze ruffled the water and, to my city eyes as the day wore on, all this seemed like a private paradise.

My angling tutor, a portly middle-aged man named Clifford, who worked for a Norwich insurance company, pulled out fish regularly – roach, perch, bream and sometimes eels of varying sizes. I caught very few because I never became much of an angler, then or during several other visits with him. In a real sense it was me who was hooked that first day – by the unique tranquillity of Fritton Lake. Without my realising it fully then, it was enough for me just to be out there on the water surrounded by all that serene natural beauty.

Victorian and Edwardian boaters at Fritton from contemporary postcards

I largely forgot about Fritton Lake over the next 30 years. After becoming a journalist with the Eastern Daily Press, I went off to work abroad as a foreign correspondent, reporting the Cold War from Berlin and Eastern Europe, and the Cultural Revolution in China. By the early 1980s I was living in London, broadcasting on the BBC World Service and writing novels. I had two young daughters, Clarissa and Lucy, who were aged four and seven, and during a summer holiday visit to Norfolk, while driving towards the coast at Yarmouth, I suddenly thought I would show my wife Shirley and my daughters the quiet lake where I once used to fish in my early teens.

To my disappointment when I found the little lane leading to the lake, a signpost directed traffic towards a larger entrance to 'Fritton Country Park' – now known as Fritton Lake Countryworld – on the main highway. There I was somewhat shocked to find a new road leading down towards the old Georgian farmhouse, and the cornfields that had previously surrounded it had been turned into a grass-covered plain, where the bright July sunlight was shimmering on the metallic roofs of hundreds of parked cars! With a sinking feeling I realised what I had once thought of as 'a private paradise' had gone very public indeed.

While I was adjusting my mind to this seemingly unpleasant fact as we drove into the car park, my two small daughters began squealing with delight – they had caught sight of the several giant red wooden 'mushrooms' dotted around a very big and attractive children's adventure playground that had been laid out beside the farmhouse. Tempting tree walks, obstacle-course climbing frames, sandpits, enclosed 'snake' slides and larger-than-life wooden elephants and camels dotted the area, and on the lawns leading down to the lake dappled ponies were being mounted and ridden under supervision by other excited youngsters like themselves.

On the lake families were sculling around in rowing boats or propelling pedalo craft with their feet, others were enjoying picnics in the woods and windsurfers in wet suits were scudding across the water clinging to their bright sails. The secluded Fritton I had known at the age of fourteen, had, it was quite clear, been caught up in the 'leisure revolution' and was proving as popular with parents holidaying with their children as it had once been to anglers seeking quieter, more solitary pleasures.

My daughters gleefully joined the great throng on the imaginatively designed adventure playground, then queued up to ride the ponies down to the lake and back, once, twice and a third time. In a quite different way they were finding Fritton Lake and its environs as enchanting as their father had done 30 years earlier.

The formal gardens and the wooded borders of the lake, we found as we wandered through them, had lost none of their charm and, as my dismay at the many changes lessened, I began to realise that the presence of throngs of visitors did little or nothing to diminish Fritton's great natural beauty.

This impression was enhanced greatly when I discovered that there were three cottages and a former coach house that could be rented for holiday visits all year round. I first returned alone to stay a week in one of the cottages and fish, and in the early mornings and evenings before and after the gates were opened to the public, the lake and its surrounding woods remained as quiet and seemingly private as they were in the 1950s.

It was to be the first of many visits and in this tranquil setting, in about 1983, I spent a very special day's fishing with my father Alfred whom I had not seen for about 40 years. My parents had been

divorced when I was only two, and he lived nearby in
Lowestoft, where I finally sought him out during one
Fritton visit. He died not long after that rare day
together on the lake.

It was during my first stay at Fritton and later two-
week family holidays by the lake that I met Walter
Mussett and learned how he had graduated from his
role as Lord Somerleyton's gamekeeper to becoming
the creator and manager of the modern Fritton Lake
Country Park. We quickly became friends, and with
great relish Walter told me stories of Fritton's history,
and his own happy experiences there.

'You should write your life story, Walter,' I said
casually one day, little realising that some 20 years
later I would be publishing it among books put out by
my own new Norfolk-based publishing imprint.

In fact, after deciding to leave London in the late
1990s and return to live in Norfolk, I was able to lease
the Old Coach House and enjoy a long uninterrupted
spell close to the lake. Whilst there I decided to fulfil
a long-standing ambition to become a publisher as
well as a writer and a book celebrating the beauty of
Fritton Lake and Walter Mussett's life-long
connections with it became a natural priority.

I had worked with Keith Skipper when we were
both fledgling reporters on the *Eastern Daily Press* in
the 1960s and, because he had become in the
intervening years a celebrated writer on local Norfolk
matters, it was obvious that he would be the best

possible man to help guide this story gently into print. So I was delighted when he accepted my invitation to become its author.

What follows then is the culmination of all these strands of personal affections and local history. Research in local archives suggests that the original name of Fritton may be derived from Freya, the Scandinavian goddess of beauty and love. It is not difficult to imagine gods and goddesses besporting themselves in and around such a glorious and placid stretch of water, perhaps justifying the appellation 'fabulous' which always springs to my mind whenever I think of Fritton.

So, for me – and I am sure this goes for Walter Mussett too – Fritton Lake remains one of the loveliest areas of natural beauty in Britain and indeed the world. Out on the water it is easy to imagine you are in a Norwegian fjord or in Canada's far west. The lake is a source of rare pleasure to all who visit it, and the main purpose of this book is to chronicle and celebrate something of that rarity – and, through Walter's affectionate life-long devotion to Fritton Lake, share it with all who read this story.

Anthony Grey is the international best-selling author of the novels Saigon, Peking, Tokyo Bay *and the autobiographical memoir* Hostage in Peking. *He founded The Tagman Press in Norfolk in 1998.*

Walter Mussett

CHAPTER ONE
EARLY DAYS

First impressions can be misleading, but in the case of Walter Mussett it really is a matter of what you see is what you get. A choice companion all the way from lake to lake, he commands a wide and appreciative audience for compelling stories simply told.

Gently spoken with a rural burr, and constantly ready to smile, he exudes a sense of satisfaction bordering on serenity as he mulls over so many good years in the great outdoors. A countryside upbringing may have carved a natural path to fresh air, fields, woods and water, but Walter still gives thanks for being allowed to tackle tasks perfectly suited to his talents and temperament.

During the many pleasurable visits we spent preparing this book, we strolled round his old paths on the Somerleyton and Morningthorpe estates, took a diversion or two with the RAF and even went back to the 1920s for a Norfolk childhood which was destined to set the open-air pattern of Walter Mussett's working life.

Nearly three decades on the gamekeeper's beats at two of the area's top estates, Somerleyton and Morningthorpe, gave way to a dramatic new challenge in 1969 – to run Fritton Lake, part of the Somerleyton estate on the Norfolk-Suffolk border. Walter was back in familiar territory, and it claimed him for the rest of his working days.

Falling under Fritton's unique spell, fashioned by the mirror-like surface of the water, thickly-wooded shore and countless other layers of natural beauty, has been

15

*the lucky lot of thousands over the years. Fishermen
after a handsome catch in what used to be known as
the finest pike lake in England realise there are rich
consolations even at the end of an empty line. The
sheer beauty of the place, and a rare brand of peace and
well-being, means no visit has been in vain. A stroll
among dazzling rhododendrons and azaleas, a peep
through reeds whispering old secrets and soaking up
ghostly echoes from duck decoy pipes spell
enchantment to anyone seeking refuge from the
high-speed world beyond.*

*Walter Mussett was born at White Hall Cottages
in Syderstone, near Fakenham, on October 2nd,
1922, youngest of a family of six boys. During
that same month, the BBC was formed,
Mussolini came to power in Italy, music hall
queen Marie Lloyd died at 52, David Lloyd
George was ousted as our Prime Minister and
Britain signed a treaty of alliance with Iraq. Not
that any of these big events cut much ice in the
Mussett household on the edge of the Holkham
Estate. Worries about little Walter were far more
significant. He describes his first memories.*

I spent six months of my first year in the Jenny Lind
children's hospital in Norwich with a horrible
complaint connected with my digestive system that
meant I couldn't keep anything down. Apparently, it
was most unusual for a baby to survive this problem –
so I started off as I meant to go on, looking on the
bright side and making the best of any job! The
hospital matron must have taken a shine to me

*Walter Mussett (right)
aged 3 and brother
Fred, 13, in 1925*

Alfred Mussett,
Walter's father

because she kept in touch – and even contacted my aunt when I had reached the ripe old age of 21 to wish me well on my Middle East travels!

My earliest memories of the great outdoors where I was to spend so much of my working life are of the straw lambing yards at White Hall farm, so skilfully made by hand under my father's supervision. Along one side was a double row of pens for each ewe and lambs. The yard was covered in straw with a midway gate to the pens. Wooden hurdles and poles were kept from year to year and a different field used for lambing each season. The whole scene looked very picturesque when the snow fell. A hut with tortoise stove and rough bed provided for the shepherd's needs.

When I was five, my father Alfred packed up being a shepherd and became a shopkeeper. My brother Bill took over the flock. Eldest brother Oscar rented a farm from the Holkham Estate and later bought it. Oscar's son Reg still runs Gallow Hill Farm at Burnham Market, while my brother Fred lives at Syderstone with his wife Phyllis. My brother Ernie also took up farming, while brother Reg was lost in the Dardanelles in the First World War. He was a

keeper on the Sandringham Estate and his name appears on the Estate memorial to those who fell in the 1914-1918 conflict.

Father's small business in Syderstone saw him start as a pork butcher and he also killed pigs for other shops in the area. After a year or so he changed to greengroceries and confectionery, apparently a popular move. There were only five wireless sets in the village and so a loudspeaker was put up in the shop and people came in during the evenings to hear what was going on. Saturday was the biggest draw as folk filed in eagerly for the football results and to check their coupons. Plenty of fruit, chocolate and cigarettes changed hands. I recall 20 Players cost 11d (just under 5p in modern money) while a packet of 5 Woodbines set you back tuppence.

Syderstone School group, 1930, with Walter second from the right on the second row from the back

Goods arrived by lorry, and when I was seven, a wheelbarrow was made for me to play an important part in the delivery business. After school I walked around the top half of the village and then the bottom, selling fruit and vegetables as they became available. A small money bag with float was provided and I could take up to £2 on a good run. I was paid three shillings (15p) in the pound. It's worth remembering that farm wages then were 30 shillings a week. I enjoyed my time as a Norfolk barrow boy – plenty of fresh air and a few pennies to spend – but when the weather was wet or rough it became a bit more of a chore.

Tragically, my mother Charlotte fell ill with cancer and died when I was seven. I was sleeping out at a neighbour's house and can remember going home to breakfast one morning and father telling me Mum had gone. I ran out into the garden and shed a few tears. I knew things would never be the same again, and I was right. No-one can take the place of your mother at that age. The schoolmaster at Syderstone added to my sorrows when the church bell tolled. He blurted out, 'Is that for your mother?' I could have run out of class but gritted my teeth and stood firm. On mother's funeral day I was sent to White Hall farm with my nephews Derrick and Bill. The following day I helped my brother Fred to put the wreaths back on her grave in Syderstone churchyard. They had been placed in the church porch for the night. As a sort of consolation after this harrowing time, I had a new bike. I'd learned to ride on an old one.

A near neighbour, Katherine Edge and her son Peter moved in to look after us when Mum died. Mrs Edge, a widow, acted as housekeeper and mother-figure and remained with our family until Father passed on in 1949. I got on particularly well with Peter, who was a bit younger than me, and we biked to school together. He also finished up working on the Somerleyton Estate as a farm foreman. Father picked up a contract to deliver fruit and vegetables to Bircham Newton aerodrome, but it wasn't easy going in a pony and cart.

My brother Fred, ten years older, had deep litter white leghorn chickens in 1930 and used a hurricane lamp that worked on paraffin to provide extra light and heat in the old barn he had converted into a chicken shed. These were pioneering days for deep litter ventures, with up to a foot of chaff and shavings spread out on the floor for the chickens to scrap about in. Fred enclosed mangers that had been used for cattle and turned them into nest boxes.

There was a lot of unemployment at this time and men were on what we called 'pay and work' for very little, grafting in stone pits, throwing the stones from ledge to ledge and then out of the top. No cash was given, but pay vouchers could be handed to the shopkeeper for provisions; no chocolate or cigarettes were allowed to be exchanged for these slips. I remember being in the shop when a man strolled in and said: 'Can I have a packet of fags or some tobacco?' Father would have to say no but then he might add: 'If you could help in the garden, digging

or whatever, I can find you something for doing that.' Word got round and we soon had more gardeners than we needed!

Father had lots of expenses, especially when Mum fell ill and needed operations and constant care, so what money we had soon diminished. We eventually moved out of the house and he went back to looking after sheep for a tenant on the Raynham Estate. I biked to Helhoughton School, about three miles away, and a bull was occasionally ready to greet us on the meadow we had to cross. I never did like those animals! Well, when we were at White Hall and visiting Leicester Square nearby, one chased our cart and really frightened me. I was only four at the time and mighty relieved to get home in one piece after this ordeal.

My close links with the Somerleyton Estate began when my father moved there for a six-week lambing stint. We enjoyed being near the coast and having a garden, but there was a lot of work to be done. I pushed a barrow to dump waste on Saturday mornings, a mile each way for thrippence. Then I found a better job for a whole shilling, working from 9am until noon

Alfred Mussett and Katherine Edge at lambing time

with the head gamekeeper, Fred Chapman. A kind man who had been gassed in the first world war when he won the Military Medal, he pointed me in the right direction as I gave some thought as to what I might do after leaving schooldays behind. It's worth pointing out that in those days it was customary to

21

call all department heads on the Estate 'Mr' rather than by their first name. So for me it was always 'Mr Chapman' rather than 'Fred'.

Somerleyton Hall

When young Walter forged his first fruitful links with the Somerleyton Estate, little did he realise just how big a role it was destined to play in his working life. The estate and hall, an elegant Victorian country house with 12 acres of gardens, was built by a wealthy railway contractor, Sir Morton Peto, who in 1863 sold it to Sir Francis Crossley (great-grandfather of the present Lord Somerleyton) to pay off his gambling debts. The present Lord Somerleyton inherited the title in 1959. His father served with the Ninth Queen's Royal Lancers until 1924, achieving the rank of Major and winning the Military Cross in the First World War. He inherited the title in 1935 – and so was there to welcome Walter Mussett to the Somerleyton ranks a year or so later.

When I left Somerleyton School at Christmas, 1936, I started work on Kitty's Farm which supplied milk, cream, butter and cheese to Somerleyton Hall. My main job was to churn the butter and take items to the Hall. I also gave a hand to Sam Cole, the stockman, carting feed around, a tasty mixture of sliced mangold, swedes and hay. I also recall having to take coke to the Hall. Someone usually managed to ring about ten minutes before leaving off time. A load was required, so I had to bag it up, cart it there with pony and trolley, a four-wheeled flat job, and then tip the bags out and slide them down the stoke-hole. No easy task, but at least it was a two-man job – or a man and a boy. And I was that boy!

In those days there were 20 servants in the Hall and 22 in the gardens, a groom and two stable-lads, and three chauffeurs. As they retired they weren't always replaced, and the number of staff gradually went down.

One day Lord and Lady Somerleyton, two of the most thoughtful people on earth, said it was high time I had a change. They offered me a choice – Hall Boy, in the gardens or the carpenter's shop. I had a day or two to think it over. The Hall appealed to me most, but father said this was 'no place for a boy among all them mawthers!' Then another offer came along. Jimmy Darkin was retiring and the gamekeepers needed a boy. After that spell of working with Fred Chapman, I had no hesitation in accepting.

Lord & Lady Somerleyton at a meeting of the Norwich Staghounds before WWII

Outdoor adventures beckoned. I was introduced to the beat keepers, Bill Rumsby, a proper Norfolk man on Home Beat; Billy Saunders, slightly younger than the others on Wickerwell Beat; Jack Morley on Herringfleet Beat and, finally, Fred Ollett on Decoy Beat who was later to become my father-in-law when I married his daughter Peggy. There were five keepers and a boy, two full-time warreners and two

who worked in the woods in summer and rabbit-catching in autumn and winter. There were 16 people working on estate maintenance, ten were employed in the wood and another eight at Kitty's Farm.

Fred Ollett, Walter's future father-in-law

My first day was spent on the rearing field preparing coops for hens and young chicks. Head keeper Fred Chapman showed me things I had to know – and I learned quickly. We had to cook eggs for pheasants at ten days old and soon rabbits were added to the feed. Hawks abounded and I was given the job of reducing their numbers by trapping them on the hill off the rearing field. This led to my being hated by the other keepers as they received an ounce of tobacco for each hawk shot! The rearing field job lasted about eight weeks. Then nest boxes had to be cleaned, creosoted and put away. I had no birds to look after in that first year but I was put on early and late duties looking at traps for warrener George Davy. By getting an early start, I was on top of the world. It meant I got time off in the afternoons and then went back on patrol in the evenings. Exactly what a keeper should do – work early and late when vermin moves. Much can be achieved that way.

Father thought it necessary for me to have a keeper's suit and had one made in Lowestoft's Bevan Street. Harris tweed, nice jacket, waistcoat, breeches and cap to match. I don't know how much it cost but I really appreciated it – even if it was too good for working in!

25

I was soon invited by the Jackson family who lived at nearby Herringfleet Hall to join ratting expeditions. Sir Thomas and Lady Jackson had two sons, Tom, two years older than me, and Julius, the same age, and a daughter, Nancy. A very homely and generous family. Corn stacks were full of rats and we would bag 50 or more in an evening, hunting with the aid of carbide gas lamps, and over 100 rats when the stacks were threshed out. We had three terriers, right little characters themselves. Jack Morley, the Herringfleet keeper had two, Jip and Jan, and they seemed to know exactly where to go for rats. One would go round the shed while the other ventured inside and put creatures out it didn't catch. I remember a dog got stuck in a rib roller, an implement for breaking up hard patches of soil, and we had one heck of a job getting it out.

I had a new bike for work when I left school. It cost £3, but now I set my heart on a new model, a Raleigh with hub dynamo at £8. Father coughed up and I repaid him partly when I could. The old bike had to carry huge loads, traps and so on, and one day Mr Chapman loaded three dozen each on the handlebars and in bags on the back. One got in the wheel on Somerleyton Church Hill. Up goes Wally and comes down in the road. No injuries – but the poor bike! I counted 11 spokes broken and the valve flattened. Off we went to Woodcock's bicycle shop for repairs. It was back in service the next day.

Christmas 1937 marked my first year completed on the Somerleyton Estate. All workers met at the Hall in the morning and received festive greetings from Lord and Lady Somerleyton along with warmest thanks for all efforts during the past year. We were invited in for sherry and mince pies and received a cash gift according to our pay. There were plenty of characters on the scene. Ernie Brown, head man in the carpenter's shop, was called Concrete Brown. He arranged for wooden posts around Somerleyton Green to be removed and concrete, made on the Estate, put in place. He was good at monologues – Kissing Cup being a favourite at local concerts – and two of his sons were at school with me. An older son worked in the office of Captain Walter Flatt, the Estate Agent and a gentleman I admired very much.

Changes on the keeping front kept me on my toes. Jack Morley went as Head Keeper to the Sotterley Estate. Bill Saunders went to West Norfolk. George Simpson, a replacement from Six Mile Bottom, took on Herringfleet and Bob Coe, who lodged with Estate thatcher Billy Fisher, took on Wickerwell Beat.

After the shooting season we all went rabbiting. Tenants were invited for a day or two of shooting. Hundreds of rabbits were killed but it made little difference for there were even more the following year. This was before myxomatosis. No foxes were taken, although Billy Rumsby and I took a badger by mistake. At the age of sixteen I was given Herringfleet Beat to look after when George Simpson left after only a year.

Then, on Sunday, September 3rd, 1939, Neville Chamberlain came on the wireless to tell us we were at war with Germany.

CHAPTER THREE

FRITTON AT WAR

In the early days of the Second World War, the invasion of Britain was a very real threat. East Anglia, geographically close to occupied Europe, was certain to be a target area. Four days after the German invasion of Holland, on the evening of May 14 1940, the Secretary of State for War, Anthony Eden, made an important radio broadcast in which he pointed out that Europe had been overrun by German parachutists. To prevent such a thing taking place in Britain, a new special force was being formed. The name of the new force – Local Defence Volunteers – described its duties in three words.

After war was declared the Local Defence Volunteers, LDV, forerunner of the Home Guard, were formed with an Auxiliary Fire Service, AFS, at Somerleyton. I joined them as a messenger boy. It wasn't long before we had the odd bomb around. We were told they were trainee pilots – bound to hit and miss! I was part of a team of four on duty one night in five – LDV Joe Smith, warden Harry Wilson, First Aider Ernie Firman and AFS 'stalwart' Walter Mussett. The Fearless Four were ready for action.

A string of delayed action bombs once fell at Fritton at night on my beat. I was out with dogs and gun at about 6.30 am. I ventured through Sandy Lane, left my dogs and bike and walked to a mound. I moved on to a second mound when about 150 yards in front of me there was an almighty bang and a whole oak tree was blown thirty feet up in the air. I got out fairly quick. I didn't know at the time that poor old 'Snow', that's Mr Snowling who lived nearby, was strolling to work towards the tree and the bomb. He was very shaken. I vowed not to go looking for bombs again.

The summer of 1940 saw the introduction of a highly secret underground Home Guard guerrilla movement throughout Britain. The authorities had realised that once a German invasion had been launched, no amount of road barricades or platoons of Home Guard equipped with old-fashioned guns could hope to hold off a well-trained enemy for long. Prime Minister Winston Churchill ordered Colonel Gubbins, later commander of the S.O.E., to form a force of civilian volunteers led by serving army officers to train in the art of guerrilla warfare. The job of these guerrilla bands was to take cover once the enemy invasion came, only coming out of hiding once the bulk of the enemy had moved on, leaving a small occupation force which could be picked off.

It was vital that these 'Auxiliary Units' were staffed by men who knew the landscape, the wind and the tides, and were experienced in moving about the countryside. For this reason, many farmers, gamekeepers and hunt servants were among the recruits. Security was of the utmost importance: members didn't even know the identity of those in other groups in the same district. They were trained in the use of explosives, detonators and timing devices and were given revolvers and sten guns for defensive use. Fighting knives were issued for killing individual sentries and .22 silenced rifles for carrying out assassinations if a suitable target should present itself.

An underground hideout, known as an Operational Base, was created in the dense woodland to the south of Fritton Lake, and sufficient food and equipment for 14 days was stored there. This was the anticipated useful life of the auxiliary units, and if any survived this period they were expected to revert to their civilian life to wait in the hope of a successful British counter-attack.

Not officially part of the military, the Auxiliary volunteers were outside the Geneva Convention and would certainly have been shot if captured by the enemy. On the Somerleyton estate those selected for this dangerous task included William Ward, the tenant farmer at Fritton Hall, and a young gamekeeper, Walter Mussett.

Kathleen Scott's statue at Fritton, by the lake, commemorates five local boys whose lives were cut short by the war, including Tom and Julius Jackson

The war was on in earnest. Yarmouth and Lowestoft received their share of bombs. I was asked to join the 'Guerrilla Warfare Force' to work hard preparing for a possible invasion. The Jackson boys, Tom and Julius, (my ratting colleagues) and Raymond Burrage joined me on this high-powered venture around Fritton Lake, under officer-in-charge Mr Willie Ward. My father was furious that at the age of 17 I had a Colt revolver and ammunition which I kept in my bedroom. Perhaps it was just as well we were never called into action.

To be honest, we made precious little headway digging out hides, but to be fair to us we did not get the necessary help required. Although I was in the AFS, I also had an army uniform. We were trained to use Colt revolvers and explosives with time pencils.

31

In the event of an enemy landing, it was our duty to disrupt, make things in general as awkward as possible for the invaders. During the 1940 invasion threat, it was feared that the Germans might invade from the sky using amphibious aircraft. Because of its expanse Fritton Lake was thought to be a prime location, providing space for up to 70 troop-carrying seaplanes. To prevent the enemy landing, wire hawsers were stretched across the lake at approximately 70-yard intervals.

After I joined the RAF in 1941, Fritton Lake was taken over by 'professionals' and most things changed. The Army had far more elaborate equipment than we could ever muster and did a highly efficient job after I had left the scene.

Of course, Fritton Lake, that ever-glorious stretch of water, was soon to become the focal point of my life for many years. However, I didn't know that as I became involved in the 'underground movement' in those early days of the war. Four of the five of us in our little unit became of call-up age so we left and were replaced by older men, who were most unlikely to be called up.

In 1941, Walter and Fritton were separated when he joined the RAF. We will hear more about his active service, far from home, in the following chapter. While he was away, Fritton Lake continued to play an important part in the war. In 1942 the Army requisitioned Fritton Decoy, as it was then known, for 'tank training of a most secret nature'. Its seclusion, combined with the fact that only a few people lived in the area the Army sought, made Fritton an ideal location. The Valentine amphibious tanks being tested were hidden in the woods to the south of the lake, and the camp was referred to as Fritton Bridging Camp in order to distract attention from its real purpose. These were the tanks that eventually landed so decisively in Normandy on D-Day under their own power. Winston Churchill and Field Marshal Montgomery both added distinction to Fritton by paying visits to watch this important training. No-one was allowed near the lake: even the local farmers had to have a special permit in order to gain access to their fields neighbouring the woods. Camouflage nets were used to block the view of the lake from Fritton village. Troops undergoing training were brought in to the area in the backs of covered lorries, and were not allowed to know where they were.

By late 1943 the focus of the war had shifted from a defensive position to an offensive one. Plans were made for the British invasion of occupied Europe. The Americans began to create a new air force to provide tactical support for the coming invasion, the 8th USAAF, building up its strength on East Anglian bases. On April 8th 1945 two American P47 Thunderbolts collided over Fritton Lake, whilst practising aerial manoeuvres on their return from an air-sea rescue mission. Both planes plunged into the lake. After many years of searching, parts of one of them were recovered in 1971 and exhibited at Fritton Hall. The port wing of the plane recovered from Fritton Lake was presented to the USAAF Museum at 33

Wright-Patterson Air Force base in Ohio, where it is on display. The bodies of both pilots were found and are now interred at the US military cemetery at Madingley, Cambridge.

The Auxiliary Unit was maintained until November 1944, although by then the risk of invasion had greatly diminished. The volunteers were told that 'no public recognition would be possible due to the secret nature of their duties' and that, since no written records of service had been kept, they were not eligible for the Defence Medal.

The late Lord and Lady Somerleyton with their children, Mary, Bill (the present Lord Somerleyton) and Nick during the Second World War

CHAPTER FOUR

WALTER'S WAR

After his secret 'dress rehearsal' manoeuvres around Fritton Lake, Walter volunteered for wartime aircrew duties in 1940 when he was 18. But he didn't have the necessary educational background to become a pilot or observer. He was urged to go home, attend night classes and then try his luck again. He did – and in May, 1941 joined thousands of others waiting for training. So began over five years of service to King and Country, two of them in the Middle East. But Walter's active service had a low-key beginning.

Off I went to Cardington, near Bedford, home of the ill-fated R101 airship which went up in flames in France in 1930. We were kitted out and graded – or perhaps I should call it 'degraded'! A few hundred men cutting grass with scissors ... how stupid as a first taste of RAF life. Then it was on to Skegness for six weeks of square bashing. Locals must have thought we were barmy, drilling with broomsticks because there was a shortage of rifles. A flight sergeant teaching us bayonet drill would have a red sweet in his mouth, probably a bullseye, and he would spit and claim to be spitting blood! That's how hard he wanted us to be.

Those weeks soon passed, thank goodness, and we were sent all over England, Scotland and Wales. My destination was Farnborough in Hampshire and after two or three weeks of tackling various tasks, we were told we could have a 48-hour pass. Poor Don Sutherland, a good chum, lived in Inverness and needed that long to get there! Some of us were still wondering which way to go when a train arrived full of coal, so it was on with overalls and away with the lorry to the station yard. All was not lost, for the following week we collected our reward for heaving the coal – a 72 hour pass. Our first time home in uniform, pride of the RAF. I realised this was my third wartime uniform after the AFS and LDV.

Farnborough days were mixed. I was selected with about 15 others for ceremonial duties. We looked smart, but we should have known there was a catch. 'Funeral party halt!' shouted the sergeant and off we went to Brookwood on a lorry with Union Jack and RAF flag. A sad journey repeated too many times. Coffins came from all around the country, sometimes two or three a day, with parents or girlfriends in attendance. Kenneth Farnes, the Essex cricketer, was one victim I remember well and I visited his grave since the war.

Later in life I was to lose two nephews in the RAF within six months of each other, one a pilot officer who flew from Wattisham – his parachute failed to open – and his brother, a sergeant killed in a car crash while returning to camp.

Despite the gloom of trips to Brookwood, Farnborough was an exciting place with experimental aircraft being tested on runways or catapult for Fleet Air Arm use, the Mosquito made of wood, the Boston with tricycle undercarriage. Camp dances were a big attraction and our smartness had its rewards. No trouble attracting the girls and we enjoyed having our pick. Before I joined up I had got engaged to a girl from Somerleyton – I was only 17 at the time – but she broke it off and sent my ring back while I was based at Farnborough. I can't say it bothered me too much because the girls were always plentiful!

One morning an order came for a number of us to be taken to the firing range with the Army. I was a good shot, and I was warned: 'Mussett, if you want to come back to us, don't get too many in the bull! They're looking for chaps like you for snipers.' It registered. My older brother Reg, who had worked as a keeper on the Sandringham Estate was lost in the First World War. He had been a sniper. I made sure not to get too many bulls.

I got home on New Year leave in 1942. On return to camp I noticed several of the lads were missing. They were on embarkation leave. What should I do now? After a week or two it came up on DROS – Daily Routine Orders – that volunteers were required for overseas duty. My name soon went on the list. We had an armful of inoculations, full medical and dental checks, and a pass in hand for leave. We had no idea where we might finish up. I had 14 days of pleasant leave after my arm recovered. It had been like a balloon after shots against complaints like sandfly fever and malaria. This gave some indication that the Arctic Circle was out and a nice warm place probably in store.

Leave over, it was back on the station platform at Somerleyton to say farewell to the two porters and stationmaster. From Norwich to Liverpool Street, across to Waterloo and out to Ash Vale. One day in camp and then off to Padgate for kitting out with pith helmet and khaki shorts and shirt. We set sail on St Patrick's Day, March 17th, from Liverpool to Greenock to spend a few days. Then, all of a sudden, in darkness we headed for the open seas. Some said we were heading due west when sunrise came and I'm sure we went round in circles to fool the enemy and calm ourselves. However, after two full weeks in the Atlantic, we saw land. The convoy had found a port, Freetown, in East Africa.

There were about 30 ships, convoy and escorts, and we were packed on the boat like sardines. Carpenters were still on board when we arrived at Liverpool and shavings all over the place proved they were still there. When we arrived at Freetown boys came alongside with fruit and dived for coins. Silver paper covered pennies to make them look like half-crowns, and the lads knew all the swear words in several languages! We sailed on and after another week at sea, we saw Table Mountain. Yes, it was Cape Town and we camped a few miles out of town. On arriving at Polsmoor, we met up with boys who had left Farnborough a month or more ahead of us. They were a sorry sight after having been torpedoed on the equator and spent 72 hours in the sea. Some had large sunburn scabs from neck to waist. Apparently, only two lives were lost. We thoroughly enjoyed the hospitality of the Cape Town folk and I revisited the place with my wife in 1982. Not that I recognised much of it from the time I had been there 40 years before.

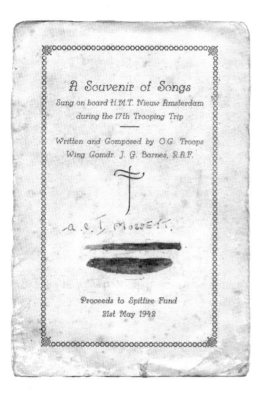

A songbook from the voyage of the New Amsterdam, *1942*

After three weeks of comparative rest, it was down to the docks where the 36,000 ton *New Amsterdam* was waiting to take us to Port Suez in the Middle East. Rommel was our main worry. He and his troops had surrounded Tobruk and were on their way. I was one of eight men detailed to light the runway at Sidi Barini for planes landing or taking off. An enemy plane would follow one of ours in and machine gun the runway. Even before take-off they would try to get to the plane on the ground. They made our job a bit hair-raising to say the least with bullets flying all around us. One night after a land mine had come down too close for comfort we ran for cover – only to be met by a sergeant with a revolver who ordered us back to our post. He was at an underground operation room which later suffered a direct hit.

I remember especially October, 1942, when the El Alamein guns opened up. What uproar! We were 20-30 miles behind the lines but had been given orders to be ready to move. With more planes and equipment at last we stood a chance of winning the war in the desert. An airstrip outside Benghazi was to be our base, and it was while we were here that a Wellington was prepared for a test flight and we were asked who would like to join it and try out the guns on a wreck just off the coast. I was one of the four who volunteered. We got ready to fire, but the plane went into a dive and never pulled out. An engineer on board saved us by pulling a wire which had broken. The plane eased out, touching treetops and hitting the runway marker. We hadn't fired a shot. No more stunt trips for me after that!

I joined the ranks of airmen going down with dysentery. With other troubles as well, I was flown to the base RAF hospital in Egypt for three weeks of treatment before moving on to Tel Aviv to convalesce. I was given a rail pass to Alexandria – Almeria, from where I had to thumb a lift for 2000 miles to rejoin my unit! Luckily, I managed to get lifts. In fact, I was back with my unit a fortnight later only to be told most had left for Italy. A visit to sick quarters set me back to square one – RAF hospital, Tel Aviv and a tour round Jerusalem, Bethlehem and the Dead Sea. I was downgraded – grade three base posting only – and celebrated my 21st birthday at Aboukir. One of the NAAFI girls happened to be 21 on the same day so the manageress ensured we had a good party. I recall the girl's name was Gladys Zillwood and we really enjoyed our double celebration very much!

Later I was posted to Air Headquarters at Cairo where I stayed until my return to the United Kingdom on the *Rio Del Pacifico* from Port Said. Although I had spent time in hospital I came home

Wartime cartoons from the Airman's Convalescent Depot at Tel Aviv

realising that many servicemen would not be so lucky. We had survived against all odds and were so proud to be part of a force which had won a major campaign of the war. My service discharge blue book states: 'An airman who at all times carried out his duties conscientiously.' I have tried to follow that through at all times of my life.

With father ill and in hospital after a fall on an icy road, I cut my RAF service short, serving at Swannington in Norfolk, Handforth

Desert graves at Hellfire Pass in Libya

in Cheshire, Eccles Road in Norfolk and RAF Warton, near Preston. I was demobbed at Henlow on August 3rd, 1946. I served for five years and despite all the dangers and hardships and the sadness of losing comrades I enjoyed seeing something of the world. Overall it was a great eye-opener for a young man who had never been outside Norfolk until then.

R.A.F. Form 2520/11

ROYAL AIR FORCE
CERTIFICATE OF SERVICE AND RELEASE

£36 Se/V/2 issued 12/8/46.

SERVICE PARTICULARS

Service Number } 1281216.   Rank L.A.C.

Air Crew Category and/or R.A.F. trade EQUIPMENT ASSISTANT.

Air Crew Badges awarded (if any). NIL.

Overseas Service 14/3/42 to 12/6/44 (MIDDLE EAST COMMAND)

R.A.F. Character V.G.   (see notes on back of certificate on opposite page)

Proficiency A SUPR   (,, '')

,, B   —   (,, '')

Decorations, Medals, Clasps, Mention in Despatches, Commendations, etc. 1939/45 STAR.
AFRICA STAR & CLASP. DEFENCE MEDAL.

Educational and Vocational Training Courses and Results NIL.

DESCRIPTION

Date of Birth 2·10·22.   Height 5'·10½'

Marks and Scars NIL

Specimen Signature of Airman N. E. Mussett.

---

of L.A.C. WE MUSSETT.
(Block Letters)

The above-named airman served in the R.A.F.V.R.
on full-time service,

from 26·5·41. to 3 AUG '46
(Last day of service in unit before leaving for release and release leave).

Particulars of his Service are shown in the margin of this Certificate.

Brief statement of any special aptitudes or qualities or any special types of employment for which recommended:—

An airman who has proved himself to be a definite asset to the good running of his unit. A hardworker who at all times has applied himself to his duties conscientiously. Conduct exemplary.

Date 3 AUG '46

Signature of Officer Commanding
SQUADRON LEADER

*RAF Certificate of
Service and Release*

CHAPTER FIVE

THE DECOY BEAT

Less than two months after returning to civilian life, Walter had got married and had taken a gamekeeper's job on the Somerleyton Estate. Given a choice of beats by Lord Somerleyton, father of the present lord, Walter went for Decoy – and he and his new wife Peggy went to live in Decoy Lodge.

Wildfowl have been a key part of Fritton Lake for several hundred years. As its former name – Fritton Decoy – suggests, it was long famous as a decoy ground for trapping large numbers of fowl for the London market. At one time there were over 20 decoy pipes situated around the lake, the last of which was employed in the early 1960s. Remains of several pipes can still be seen around the lakeside, some of which were in operation for over 250 years. By the time

A Fritton decoy in the late nineteenth century

Walter returned in the mid-1940s, Fritton Decoy was one of only five duck decoys in Britain which were still maintained in full working order. Most of the birds taken were the common wild duck, widgeon and teal, which were attracted to the lake in great numbers by the acorns in the surrounding woods.

A good year's catch for a pipe would have been between 1,000 and 2,000 ducks. The decoy consisted of a long curved dyke leading away from the water's edge for about 80 yards [73m], starting at about 18ft [5.5m] wide at its entrance and narrowing to about 3ft [1m] wide at the landward end. The whole area was covered with metal or wooden hoops and wire netting. At the narrow end was a tunnel snare net, very much like a large eel net. All along the sides were overlapping reed screens, which concealed the decoy man, but still enabled him to watch the fowl entering the pipe. They were enticed in by a highly trained, usually small and brown dog, which moved alongside the pipe on the bank luring the ducks towards the snare. The dog's resemblance to a fox, coupled with the ducks' overwhelming curiosity, eventually took the birds further and further down the pipe to the point of no return. Then the decoy man would make his appearance and force ducks into the tunnel net, from where they could be disposed of. The prevailing wind dictated which pipes were used, as ducks usually only swim or rise into the wind. Walter operated those ancient duck decoys before they were abandoned.

By the time I was demobbed I had already had a couple of years to get used to being back in England. I

Fritton decoys in the late nineteenth century

45

wouldn't say I was a different person after I came back but I had a different outlook. The war had given me the urge to travel. I felt I had seen a portion of it and would like to see more. Prior to that I had never been out of Norfolk or Suffolk. However it wasn't until quite a few years later, after I had worked at Morningthorpe and come back to Fritton as manager, that I would get the chance to fulfil my ambition of seeing more of the world.

I was lucky to come back safely to what I had known. Other young men I knew had not been so fortunate. My boyhood ratting companions Tom and Julius Jackson from Herringfleet Hall had both been killed in the war. Tom was 23 when he died and Julius 21. In the garden at Fritton today, near the lake, there is a bronze statue of a diving boy which is a memorial to Tom and Julius and three other local boys whose lives were cut short by the war. The statue was made by Lady Kathleen Scott, widow of Captain Scott of the Antarctic, who lived at Lake Cottage overlooking Fritton Lake for many years.

I had known Peggy Ollett slightly before the war. She was a local girl a couple of years younger than me. Her father, Fred Ollett, became head keeper at the Somerleyton estate while I was away in

Peggy

Walter & Peggy's wedding day

the Middle East and I met Peggy again when I came back to England just before D-Day in 1944. We struck up a friendship and it just went on from there. On 28th September 1946 Peggy and I were married at Somerleyton church. The Reverend Feast officiated and, without a honeymoon, we went to live in Decoy Lodge. I had told Lord Somerleyton that I had no knowledge of the Decoy Beat, but he said I would soon learn.

It was lovely to be back on the Estate, even if the 1947 winter was extremely cold and snowbound. In sharp contrast, the summer was very warm and I recall carrying water out for partridges. Pheasants had hatched well and most estates enjoyed a good season. But bad weather the following year brought deep concern.

Somerleyton church

I reared a few pheasants on what food we could get, mainly eggs, rabbit and biscuit meal, but it was far from easy. The method used was a hen in a coop – no run enclosure – and as a result hawks, owls, jackdaws and the odd stoat or weasel played hell with the chicks if not watched continually. When a run was attached to the coop a year or so later, life was much better, even if it did make for more work. A daily move was involved, and when that move meant from rearing field to wood and release, watch had to be kept again.

There were four, occasionally five, of us keepering with an extra boy often employed. A bonus of thrippence a duck was paid to me at the end of each season.

Decoy Lodge

I enjoyed these years on Decoy Beat although it was hard work for all the family. My father-in-law's experience as a decoy man helped a lot. Our two sons John and Gordon were born in December, 1947 and May, 1950. They were at work on odd jobs as soon as they were able. A very quiet approach to a decoy is most important, so after dark on winter evenings, pipe paths had to be kept clean, raked clear of sticks or swept clear of snow. We all got busy by the light of the tilley lamp. I was most lucky to have a gamekeeper's daughter as my wife!

During my years at the decoy I recall how ice had to be broken to get to water around the pipes. A pipe was the old method of catching wildfowl. The famous naturalist Peter Scott [son of Lady Kathleen Scott] once lived in Lake Cottage on the opposite side of the lake and just past the fourth pipe. This was rebuilt in 1935-36 by an army of workers with just wheelbarrows, picks and shovels. Work had been in progress on the waterworks and the noise had sent ducks up the lake away from the decoy area. So an old site of the pipe was reopened. However, with new wood and netting the fowl didn't take to it. Then the war came along and it was all out of bounds while the lake was used for amphibious tank training.

*Walter Mussett
with his dog*

I loved the lake and the ducks and all the rare birds that came. Getting ducks into the decoy looked easy, but it wasn't. As often as not something put them off. Maybe a twig cracked, maybe a sudden panic for no reason. One day it was a sparrow hawk which flew out of the pipe as soon as I got there. You never knew what you would catch in those pipes. I caught jay, herons, kingfishers, and even snipe and woodcock. The pipes worked best with a north-west or north-west-by-west wind. The ducks won't wear an east wind. You know the old saying 'When the wind is in the east 'tis good for neither man nor beast.' Well, that goes for ducks too.

I started decoying in October and went right on until the end of January unless Lord Somerleyton wanted a duck shoot round about Christmas. Then I packed up. Decoying and shooting don't go together. Ducks

must have peace and quiet. It was night-and-day work but I wouldn't have changed that job for anything.

Walter Mussett at Decoy Lodge

Many books have been written about decoys, but I am one of the last people to have worked one, helping with it from 1937 until 1960. By that time the birds were caught mainly for release in the London parks or for ringing and release. After the pipes stopped being used they were kept in working order for a few years, but as the maintenance was expensive they gradually fell into disrepair. It would be more than 40 years before I was to be involved with a decoy again.

The lake is very deep in parts, and full of secrets. A fascinating area, especially after catching good-sized eels and pike up to 21 pounds. I've seen 32-pound whoppers caught. One winter when I hadn't long

Ducks swimming towards the mouth of a decoy

been back at Fritton, they took 443 pike, all of them over 15 pounds, from the stretch of water below Fritton Old Hall. I made wire netting cages for Lord Somerleyton to catch eels which were given to

Driving ducks down the pipe

friends or sent to
London to be smoked.
One day I was about to
visit a cage trap when
Lord Somerleyton
arrived to tell me about
a large branch which
had fallen across a ride
and was to be left there.
We went by boat to
inspect but no eels were
caught. However, in the
last cage were four or five lovely tench. They were
taken in a tank on the Land Rover to the Hall
gardens pond and flourished there for several years.

Harvest time

You never knew what would turn up on the lake or
in the woods. We had an osprey one year. He was up
on the common day after day, and you could see him
fishing in the lake almost any time. He used to drop
from the sky like a bullet and take big fish out of the
water like a flash.

Shelduck would nest in the heather and occasionally
we would rear a few by hand. Those that hatched
would then take their young down to the lake and
after a while across country to the river or finish up
on Breydon Water near Yarmouth. Old birds would
fly around while the young ran. One time we were
cutting a tree down a yard or two away from an old
shelduck's nest – we didn't know she was sitting
there, of course – and then when the tree fell it came
down crack on top of her! She kept right on sitting

on her eggs, and they hatched out safe enough. She
deserved a medal, that bird. But today very few
shelduck, if any, nest on Ashby Common.

Peggy took up bean picking, turkey plucking and
housework for Mr Hemming at Mill House. He had
lost his wife and was retired with two grown-up sons.
I arranged to make use of his meadow for chickens
and it was soon set up with huts and extra wire. So
began Peggy's sideline – egg production.

After several years with good sport and fair numbers,
I considered tips of £8 or £9 per season to be on the
low side. The head keeper took two-thirds, the rest
being divided between the other three or four of us.
Well, just like Oliver Twist I asked for more and
brought the subject up with Lord Somerleyton. Much
to my surprise he agreed with me, but pointed out
this was how it had been for years; it would seem
unfair to change it. However, this was not the end of
the matter. Captain Flatt, the estate agent, came
down for a discussion which ended with me being
offered the old mill and buildings to rent at £7.10s per
year with full agreement of Lord Somerleyton and
Sir Edmund Bacon, at that time a trustee of the
Estate. Captain Flatt was kind enough to provide
straw in return for muck, and so my pig keeping days
started with my first batch setting a healthy trend.

Things were moving fast – too fast it seemed for
some people's liking – and to add to my workload I
took on the job of secretary to the Somerleyton
branch of the British Legion. I lifted numbers from

52 to 96, and Peggy and the boys spent a lot of time waiting for me as I called on members who were sick or had other problems. Still, with hard work and willing spirits, we were winning, and eventually could afford our first car, a Standard 8 with an inside boot. It was the time of the Suez crisis and we were allowed to drive without passing a test for a while. Despite that concession, there were only three or four cars on the Estate.

There were light interludes along the way, some of them concerning his Lordship. I recall house-guests being brought down to see the Decoy. I was suffering from lumbago at the time and had a heck of a job to get up straight. As I ushered the guests round my patch I urged them to keep down low when I did as they were very interested in the work of the pipes. When we returned to the top and came out, one gentleman told his Lordship: 'No wonder his back is bad!' They had followed me all the way and done exactly as I suggested. I probably never straightened up at all. Laughter all round as the guest couldn't straighten up for a while.

Lady Somerleyton was a very kind person. I was still suffering the after-effects of service in the desert and when I felt poorly Lady Bridget said she would make appointments for me in Harley Street and the Tropical Disease Hospital. I was put on new treatment – and never looked back. Make no mistake; I wouldn't be here today without that good lady's help. The specialist concerned was invited for a day's shooting on my beat a year later and came over to see how I was getting on. I thanked him for his expert help.

I shot two foxes while at Decoy, one of each sex. Up to then no foxes had been seen at Somerleyton in living memory. Sparrowhawks were an even bigger enemy to game bags. One day I walked onto one at a pit hole. It had a partridge and had eaten one side of its breast. To my amazement, the poor bird was still alive and flinching its eyes. I had no choice but to kill it. I set a gin trap and, on returning found I'd caught a hedgehog. But I later had the sparrowhawk.

I once caught a kestrel that was nesting in the old mill, and without using a gun. She was a real terror. When old kestrels have a nest of young ones, they will take all the pheasant chicks and young partridges they can get their claws on. Just for a few weeks they are real murderers – the rest of the year they do more good than harm. I couldn't get at this old kestrel with a gun but I knew she had a nest in the top of the mill, so I sneaked up a ladder from the first floor one day, in my stockinged feet, crept along by the big beam where she had her nest, and clapped my hat on her quick before she could move. That stopped her capers. I was pleased to take her off by hand, but I wouldn't have wanted to try doing that again in a hurry.

That was over 50 years ago. Now with protection laws as they are, I watch woodpecker, thrush and a whole range of other birds being depleted. Sadly, things are not in line with nature. When five keepers,

four warrener vermin killers and a boy were
employed on the Somerleyton Estate, there were still
lots of hawks and owls around and, much to our
satisfaction, good numbers of songbirds and game.
Now I note how the likes of skylark, corncrake and
thrush have almost all gone.

You only have to look at old record books on game
where no keeper was employed to see what could be
achieved. We had our setbacks and poaching was still
in fashion. I was reminded once that without
poachers and vermin, a keeper would hardly be
needed in the first place! Having chased poachers
using cars and motorcycles, with me on foot or on a
bike, there was little chance of making a catch. Even
so, sometimes it worked out and it always gave me
great encouragement to be told that would-be
poachers, coming so close to being nabbed, had
thought better of it. One poacher admitted to taking

*The present Lord
Somerleyton on his
twenty-first birthday,
with his sister Mary and
Captain Walter Flatt*

157 birds in one season in daylight. I'm very pleased to say only a few came from my beat.

On my last day's shooting on the Estate well over 100 hen pheasants flew over Lady Bridget and the end gun with whom she was standing. It gave me immense pride to maintain a healthy stock to the end of that particular chapter. Partridges were among my favourites, although it took a lot of work to bring them up. Guns loved them in the shooting field. Gentlemen would say a 50-brace partridge day was far more enjoyable than a bag of 250 pheasants, but it meant hard work. I was never afraid of that, but sprays and chemicals beat me and many more keepers.

Around 1950 I was invited to take part in a BBC radio programme, Country Magazine, along with some well-known names of the time: Ralph Wightman, Wynford Vaughan Thomas and George Henchel with James Wentworth Day. We recorded the programme at the Stracey Arms, along the Acle Straight. All went well at my first 'appearance' and I was invited to take part in a further programme each month. The pay was £12 for half an hour – a month's wages for me at the time. In the end, though, I only took part in that one recording.

Lord Somerleyton died in July 1959, and, of course, things were never to be the same. His son, the present Lord Somerleyton, came to see me and explained his plans for the future. I simply could not agree then to my role in them. I had put in a request for our house

to be modernised, with water and electricity to be laid on, but our pleas fell on deaf ears. We badly wanted to modernise our home, mainly for the benefit of our growing boys, and after a long discussion with my wife, the decision was made that it was time to move on.

Gordon and John Mussett

So I made up my mind to leave Somerleyton at the end of the season. It was no trouble for me to obtain references which I kept until I retired. Lady Bridget begged me to stay – but still gave me an outstanding reference. When I returned nine years later, she said how pleased she was to see me, Peggy and the boys back on the Estate. I had six or seven interviews and was allowed to choose where the Mussett wagon would next come to rest.

So, after 14 years on the beat at Somerleyton, Walter and family moved to the Morningthorpe Estate in an area tucked away in charming lanes a mile or so from the main Norwich-Ipswich road leading into Long Stratton. The Sargent family had taken over in about 1912 when Cecil Sargent became tenant. He purchased the property in 1918 and was succeeded by his son, Cyril and, in turn, Cyril's son Hugh. The farm comprises some 2000 acres and extends from Morningthorpe and Fritton (yes, another one! It seems Walter and 'Fritton' are synonymous) into nearby parishes. It was Cyril Sargent who extended the invitation to Walter to take over from his retiring keeper. He had known Walter since he started his gamekeeping career. Sadly, Cyril died before the switch was made and Walter went to work for Hugh who had taken over from his father.

Cyril Sargent

Although Cyril had gone – and he really knew what a keeper's job involved – his son Hugh and his wife Bridget made us very welcome, and we are still firm friends today. They have four sons, Michael, Anthony, David and Christopher, who was born after we arrived.

Hugh and Bridget knew what it was all about and we got on very well. Bridget Sargent's father, Mr Giles Tuker, was a big help in many ways. He had a fruit farm in Essex and often brought back apples for use in the woods; the birds loved them and a few in the snow would keep pheasants happy at home.

I saw my first year at Morningthorpe in 1960
as a chance to put on a show. It was a kind
summer and everywhere that had some game
saw partridges doing well. I was shown
round the Estate by Mr Mathewson, the
73-year-old keeper, and this was a real eye-
opener. He had been keeper at Shotesham
during the First World War. He wasn't short
of a bob or two. He owned two houses and
once bought a farm with ready cash, complete
with stock and implements! He told me he
once had a bath full of half-crowns (twelve
and a half pence) under his bed. One day the
shopkeeper told him his son often had money
to spend and bought sweets and other items for other
boys. He found the money came from his bath
account – so he put a stop to that and his son had to
work a long time without pay.

Bertie Mathewson

Mr Mathewson eventually gave up farming and
bought some houses. He lived in one of them without
any amenities like electric cooker or television. I
asked his wife if she'd like a TV set. 'Chance would
be a fine thing!' she replied. Then the old boy
chipped in; 'You don't want one o' them noisy
things ... got enough troubles around us without
others from around the world.'

He had a daughter, Betty, who picked currants with
my wife Peggy. Betty could draw a dial and tell the
time by the sun within five minutes of the actual
time. Once she worked by moonlight to get in the
swede and mangolds – so she could tell time by the

Morningthorpe Manor

moon as well! The old boy taught me a lot. In 1962 he showed me how both hen and cock French partridge sit on a nest about five yards from each other. As we walked by the stream, which he called the beck, he would show me where a stoat and rats had been; he could tell by marks in the mud.

I recall my first shoot when several familiar faces were there – Lord Somerleyton (with my father-in-law, Fred Ollett), Mr Bob Formby, Mr Donald Steward and Mr John Buxton. We had 222 head by lunch, enough to set the pace, but the rains came to prevent another shot being fired. We had the privilege of walking over lots of adjoining land with beaters and others on several farms. Birds had been fed in a number of locations and this really helped. Fox shoots were organised with local landowners,

*Manor bungalow,
Morningthorpe*

favourite haunts being Hardwick
Airfield and Crow Green, both off the
Estate but haunts of some cunning old
foxes.

Back to the start of our Morningthorpe
adventure. We had a bungalow opposite
the boss – but no worries there. I worked
hard and to the best of my ability. But
what to do about all the rats? The old
keeper suggested zinc phospherine, and
showed me how to prepare it. His moustache was
covered in poison! I kept wondering if he would
survive. Well, he did – mainly to warn me to be very
careful as the stuff was so strong. I wore a face mask
and took all precautions. The rats were sorted out.
His son was keeper on an adjoining farm at Bayland
Hall Estate. One of the Bayfield family had been a
keeper there when it belonged to a different family.
We got on well, but he decided to have a change and
moved to Cockley Cley near Swaffham. After that it
was made one Estate of Morningthorpe and Bayland.

Hugh Sargent

We used mainly BOCM pheasant feed starter pellets. Old keepers were most reluctant to rely on modern feeds. When I started all chicks had to be treated with powder and a pair of bellows; the birds almost went mad in with the hen. Treated water was also used and

Walter Mussett

incubators were fumigated. Stubborn old keepers wouldn't use incubators, but I'd been shown their value at Somerleyton by Mr Chapman. This knowledge paid off for me at Morningthorpe. David Beamish came to Bayland and we got on well, with 300-plus on both grounds on first day pheasant shoots. He had been at Somerleyton with me. In fact, he started work there on leaving school.

Sadly, partridges declined throughout East Anglia and pheasants had to take their place. I thought a few ducks would be a good idea, and Mr Tuker agreed. We prepared without much success, but all was not lost. A dragline was brought in and ponds dug. These have provided lots of sport since the mid-1960s.

Peggy passed her driving test and our son John left school to start with Young's Builders as an apprentice carpenter. Meanwhile our other boy Gordon shone at pole vaulting in school competitions and finished first

David Beamish

in Norfolk in his age group. He came third in the All-England Schools Sports, quite an achievement.

Miss Sybil Harker was a big help in providing a fibreglass pole for his use, and she showed many other acts of kindness.

Many changes took place during my spell at Morningthorpe. We became more or less a larder for foxes, and some poaching took place. We were able to control this but not cut it out completely because as soon as one was caught someone else would start. Fowl pest cut us down to size, and I owe special thanks to all who supported me through trying times.

Time seemed to fly, and after nine enjoyable seasons at Morningthorpe I began thinking about another change. It seemed I had got as far as I was going to get in the gamekeeping field, and a fresh challenge certainly appealed to me. The boys had left school and taken up apprenticeships. I had been a keeper for 30 years. Now the big question was how I would cope with any dramatic change of direction.

To my utter surprise, I discovered that the tenancy of Fritton Hall and the surrounding farm was about to be given up by Willy Ward who had been there for 60 years – a remarkable record. With the farm he had the right to let out fishing boats on the lake. Willy had been there since 1908, and was due for a well-earned retirement. I had known him since 1936, and he had led our guerilla warfare band at the beginning of the war.

In my keepering days at Fritton I had sometimes dreamed of running the place myself one day. The late Lord Somerleyton and I had even spoken of it one day just after the war. I often used to take him on the lake in a rowing boat to go after a brace or two of ducks which he would keep for his own table. One morning, as we were rowing past the Fritton Lake gardens, I said something like 'I'd like to have that place', and he replied 'Well, one day maybe you will!'

I spoke to Mr Sargent and Mr Tuker about the possibility of making a change. They didn't want me to leave, which was quite flattering, and I was offered the same pay to stay at Morningthorpe as I anticipated getting at Fritton. I mulled it over and came to the conclusion that the challenge and change were attractive to me, my wife and my sons. So I applied to take over at Fritton and to be reunited with my beloved lake. To my amazement, I soon heard that my claims were being seriously considered.

I asked if I could lease the lake and develop it further as a family attraction. As a result of this request, I went to the offices of Savills the estate agents in Norwich for talks with their man, Mr Turnbull, and Lord Somerleyton. After putting my views across, I was asked to wait outside the office. I hardly had a chance to sit down before they called me back inside. Would I like the job of manager of Fritton Lake rather than leasing it? This meant no initial outlay of money on my part at all, but a salary and a bonus, depending upon how successful I might be.

Well, I was almost dizzy with excitement! Surely this

was the challenge I needed, and I really knew that when I went home to think over the offer I was on my way home to Fritton Lake. Lord Somerleyton had asked me how much rent I'd be prepared to pay for the lake. 'A couple of thousand' I suggested. 'Good heavens!' he exclaimed, 'just how do you intend to raise that?' I told him by attracting sufficient numbers of visitors through the gates. He must have liked my style because that was when I was offered the manager's post.

I still had a winter's shooting ahead of me at Morningthorpe. This had to be fully completed in order to leave in good faith. It all went reasonably well, but the biggest problem was finding someone to take my place. Perhaps I could have left and not bothered, but I wanted to see things sorted out properly. A fresh keeper moved in. Now I could resume my travels – although this time it was just like going home.

Fritton Lake from the air

SOMERLEYTON HALL,
LOWESTOFT.

September 12ᵈ

———.

Dear Walter.

Thank you for your letter
which I was very pleased to
receive. I can certainly say
that we shall be delighted
to have you and Peggy back
on the Somerleyton Estate. I
also feel sure that you will make
a great success of the job after
the teething troubles are over.

I am glad that you have

*Letter from Lord
Somerleyton*

been over to see Mr and Mrs Ward.
and have found them helpful.

Yes, I would like you to come
over to move the boats from
the water in October, provided
Mr Sargent is agreeable. I do not
wish to inconvenience Mr and
Mrs Sargent in anyway.

I shall ask you to come over
to meet me from time to
time during the winter and
will probably be asking you
to come over to meet Mr
Ward and myself before
Michaelmas. Yours sincerely
Somerleyton

CHAPTER SEVEN

BACK TO THE LAKE

After nearly three decades as a gamekeeper, Walter took up a daunting new challenge in 1969 – to run Fritton Lake as a country park attraction on the Somerleyton estate. Of course, he was back on a familiar beat, but knew full well this would prove a really tough examination, albeit in glorious surroundings. He took the job on condition that if it didn't work out either way after two years, he'd call it a day.

Walter and Peggy moved into Fritton Hall, the house which stands at the entrance to the Country Park, and ran it as a guest house. Originally the manor house of the Fritton estate, and quite separate from the Somerleyton estate by which it is now owned, parts of the building are believed to date from the 17th century. From the 1860s onwards the Hall was let out to tenant farmers, and even became a 'Temperance Hotel' for a few years in the early 1900s. When Fritton officially became a Country Park in 1976 the Hall was divided to form the restaurant and the manager's house.

Between 1905 and 1967 the park was used to farm sugar beet and mixed crops, including top-quality barley which was sent to the local brewery to make whisky. A model farm, with pigs, cows, horses and chickens together with a dairy, barn, mangold store and cart shed was built around 1870. By Walter's time the farm buildings had fallen into disrepair but, thanks to a grant from the Rural Development Commission, they re-opened as the heavy horse stables in 1993.

Fritton Lake is part of the Norfolk Broads, excavated

Fritton Lake.

in the twelfth century to obtain peat. The lake covers
170 acres [69 ha] and is about two and a half miles
long. At its western end, the deepest part, it has 12 ft
[3.6 m] of clear water, 6 ft [1.8 m] of mud and peat
and then brushwood deposits to the hard valley floor at
34 ft [10.4 m]. In 1850 there was an island in Fritton
Lake known as Old Maid's Island, but this is now
permanently submerged. In 1885 the lake was
connected to reservoirs constructed at Lound via
underground pipes. It was not until 1930 that water
was extracted from the lake in any large measure. As a
reservoir for the East Anglian Water Company, it
supplied an average of two million gallons of high
purity water daily.

There is a long history of pleasure boating as well as
fishing on Fritton Lake. Tenant farmers from as long

Edwardian boating

ago as the late 19th century hired out boats for visitors to enjoy the beauty of Fritton's natural surroundings. Visitors to Yarmouth loved Fritton Lake – billed in Edwardian times as 'the prettiest of all the Broads' – and came there in droves, transported by the Great Eastern Railway to nearby St Olave's station, by horse and carriage, and most of all by bicycle. But by 1969 the tradition of pleasure boating on the lake had all but ground to a halt, and reviving it was one of Walter's first tasks.

Fritton Lake Country Park logo devised by Walter Mussett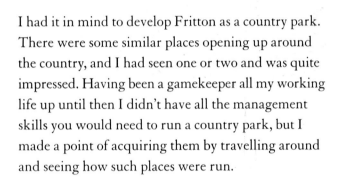

I had it in mind to develop Fritton as a country park. There were some similar places opening up around the country, and I had seen one or two and was quite impressed. Having been a gamekeeper all my working life up until then I didn't have all the management skills you would need to run a country park, but I made a point of acquiring them by travelling around and seeing how such places were run.

Some people wrote us off from the start. 'They'll be gone well inside two years' they prophesied glumly. But we were used to hard work over long hours. We opened the guest house at Easter and we were soon fully booked and passing on bookings to the Corner House and others. This went on for three years, and then we concentrated on the day trade – a move that paid off handsomely.

The scene that greeted us when we returned to Fritton wasn't what you would call lively. There were a few fishing boats on the lake, rather dilapidated. No pleasure boats at that time. But the garden was fairly

71

attractive. One reason why I accepted the post of manager at Fritton rather than becoming its tenant was the fact that so much money was needed to replace the boats and repair the house, and I would have had to borrow it. It would have cost the earth.

With a staff of three at the start, we were limited in what we could do. An old fashioned loo worked with a penny in the door. The bucket had to be changed to a flushing system. There were vending machines for drinks, snacks and cigarettes, and machines to give change. These had to go at the end of the first season, with cups and saucers, pots of tea and cakes bought in for a start. I felt that having more people around the place, rather than machines, would create a happy atmosphere – and that was what we wanted.

The family and staff of Somerleyton Hall and Fritton Lake in the 1970s. Walter Mussett is seated third from the left in the front row, next to Lady Bridget

On the lake, we had five new fibreglass rowing boats and added to them each year. More room was needed for parking cars. I wasn't impressed by our first year. Numbers were low, but there had been no facility to cater for coaches. Gardener George Peake and his wife Madie were part of the set-up when we arrived, and they were a great help in getting us on the rails. So was Stella Turner on the entrance gate. No cash registers here – just a money bowl! Yes, a lot of alterations were needed. Fishing took priority but algae on the water put this in doubt, and rowing boats were let by the hour.

The new boats

When windsurfing was introduced on the lake it proved a real hit. It grew rapidly, but more algae on the lake curtailed the use of boards. Unhelpful publicity, some of it not entirely accurate, put many off this sport.

Gradually more people got to hear of Fritton Lake and what it had to offer. Lots of grass had to be cut by hand and extra flower beds made. Women's Institutes, Silver Thread clubs and other visitors loved colour and we had to bear things like this in mind if we were serious about making headway.

73

The gardens

Development had to come, although it was a dirty word to some minds. A parish meeting was called to air objections to plans for any kind of expansion at Fritton Lake. Caravans and things like that would simply bring more people and cars into Fritton, it was claimed. Locals were reminded how some change was inevitable, and it would be for the better if it was carried out by the Somerleyton Estate itself rather than by some other company. Views were frankly exchanged.

I had no doubts that I was presiding over a growing enterprise in a tasteful and careful manner, and it was a great pleasure to see satisfied smiles on the faces of visitors of all ages. And I liked to think that locals who had doubts about expansion came to see this country park as a well-run and attractive amenity in their midst.

For the first time in our lives together Peggy and I were able to take an annual holiday and we took the opportunity to go overseas – my ambition since I had been in the RAF. The first year we were back at Fritton we went to Jersey, and the next year to Switzerland. It was only £50 each. Later we visited California, Florida and South Africa, among other places.

The official opening by Lord Kennett of Fritton Lake Country Park in 1976 was the cue for several other attractions in Norfolk and Suffolk to take the competition seriously. I was helped considerably by an extra consultant, Norman Hudson. There were times when I would have liked to have moved faster, but no doubt it was right to hold back on occasions. I kept looking over my shoulder to see who was catching up and might soon be passing us. Contact was made with other attractions to pool ideas and work together wherever possible, especially in the distribution of posters and leaflets. The big idea didn't last long, but Fritton advertised and worked together with Kessingland Wildlife Park and Somerleyton Hall.

The lake contained nearly every freshwater fish except chub: huge shoals of bream, large carp – very difficult to catch – pike and roach. We laid on everything for the angler, including a tackle shop as well as boat and bank fishing. The endless armada of cabin cruisers had ruined summer fishing on the Broads, but at Fritton the only motor boat you saw was the local rescue craft. Anglers were good on the

A good catch of bream

*John Palmer and
Peter White, regular
anglers on the lake*

whole and we made many friends among those
responsible for outstanding catches. A display board
went up just outside the entrance to show what had
been achieved in recent times. We could report
catches of 500lb of bream by some Sheffield lads in
the early 1970s. 'Dodger' from Norwich landed an eel
of almost seven pounds, one of the biggest freshwater
eels ever reported caught on rod and line in the
Broads area.

There were a few ornamental pheasants around the place and rabbits and guinea pigs in runs. This picture was another soon to change. I suggested a large enclosure for water fowl and asked for a couple of ponds to be dug out. These had to be lined with clay and they worked extremely well. The ducks and geese were a credit to the place. I feel more should have been made of them for schools and educational purposes.

We were ready for all kinds of challenges. I recall a bakers' strike after a large crowd had depleted our supplies of cakes. So Peggy and daughter-in-law Jenny set to work on the home baking front. The trial run was a big success, and gradually the bought-in cakes were discontinued and our home-made produce took the honours. Baking started at 5.30a.m. in order to make enough cakes for the day. I really think that glorious smell sold them.

Walter's sons John and Gordon in 1969

More attractions followed as I continued to ring the changes. The idea for the children's adventure play area came partly from Jersey, which we had visited during our first year at Fritton. I saw an adventure playground there and thought 'That's a good idea!' In the early 1970s there was nothing like it in Suffolk or Norfolk, and hardly anything in England, so it was a real innovation. In the event it won plaudits – 'Number one in East Anglia and nearly top for the country', we were told.

Work started on the adventure playground a year or two after we moved back to Fritton. We got some other ideas from our travels in the Mediterranean and America, and looked into what could be achieved for as low a cost as possible. I knew what I wanted and didn't see why we couldn't do the same. My sons had some good ideas; John, in particular, led the way. He made a Noah's Ark out of a plug from a Wroxham

The adventure playground

The assault course

boatyard and carved a life-size elephant, camel and giraffe out of wood to go with it. Many parents and grandparents posed there with the children and sales of films went up. What could we do next? It was a case of adding something new each year, and this kept us busy. A tree walk was next to add to the fun, and slides were added with sections in fibreglass. We had a swinging bridge, and an assault course with tractor tyres hanging from chains with rope rides. The snake slides were so popular that many had to wait patiently for a turn. The giant mushrooms made of fibreglass were also a big hit with the younger children. A local firm in Oulton Broad made them up for us. Later, we added a 'flying fox' wire rope ride.

Lord Somerleyton tees off to open the pitch and putt course in 1983

The park was closed every year between October and April, which gave Peggy and me the chance to have a day off sometimes. One Sunday in the mid-70s we went to Earlham Park in Norwich and saw their pitch and putt golf course. I knew straight away we should have one at Fritton – we had a lovely setting for it alongside the lake. Of course it was expensive to lay out a really good course and it took a lot of persuasion before I was allowed to

79

go ahead. We eventually opened our 20-acre pitch and putt course in 1983, and it was a great attraction.

One bank holiday I recall seeing a queue of people waiting to get in which must have been well over 200 yards long, with people four abreast. That was when I knew we had to put in another till! Eventually we had as many as seven tills altogether, including separate ones for ice creams, the boats and the pitch-and-putt. We began the conversion of cottages, which had previously been used by farm workers, into holiday cottages. Bookings went very well in our first year of operation, 1983, and families returned year after year. Indeed, one or two who came when they were first married returned with their grandchildren. A place run properly sells itself. We had a saying that 'Fritton is the place where children bring their parents .... and just smell those cakes as you arrive!'

One person who came to stay in a holiday cottage had first visited Fritton in 1905 as a boy with his parents. He told how he had to cut his way to the edge of the lake to fish. He returned until the 1980s and then gave up driving. He died at the ripe old age of 95.

Attendance figures received so far include:	1981	1982
Beaulieu, Hants	485,415	498,840
Warwick Castle	421,000	475,000
Leeds Castle, Kent	300,587	540,650
Blenheim Palace, Oxon	339,011	310,671
Chatsworth, Derby (number of cars)	88,156	80,356
Tatton Park, Cheshire (house, garden, farm etc)	555,000	237,400
Harewood House, Yorks	230,118	229,599
Broadlands, Hants	282,795	213,872
Hever Castle	140,000	190,000
Arundel Castle, Sussex	190,970	175,814
Knebworth House, Herts	163,000	170,000
Hatfield House, Herts	146,395	151,310
Fritton Lake Country Park, Norfolk	134,431	150,000
Stratfield Saye, Hants	155,000	147,000
Blair Castle, Perthshire	100,494	102,941
Sudeley Castle, Gloucs	110,964	101,090
Lilford Park, Peterborough	80,000	88,000
Penshurst Place, Kent	83,322	82,607
Belvoir Castle, Leics	80,000	80,000
Cawdor Castle, Nairn	83,494	79,731
Bamburgh Castle, Northumberland	91,442	79,562
Ragley Hall, Warwicks	88,725	79,401
Scone Palace, Perth	89,966	78,153
Holker Hall, Cumbria	70,348	74,952
Inveraray Castle, Strathclyde	70,000	74,847
Bowood House, Wilts	47,600	69,214
Berkeley Castle, Gloucs	74,200	66,975
Glamis Castle, Tayside	75,000	66,000
Alnwick Castle, Northumberland	60,000	60,000
Newby Hall, North Yorks	55,500	56,000
Michelham Priory, Sussex	59,614	55,462
Traquair House, Peeblesshire	51,216	53,127
Hopetoun House, Scotland	46,321	46,740
Burghley House, Cambridgeshire	48,260	46,649
Elsham House, Cambridgeshire	42,600	24,200
Holkham Hall, Norfolk	38,787	38,302
Levens Hall, Cumbria	37,975	36,866
Somerleyton Hall, Suffolk	39,115	35,805
Drumlanrig Castle, Dumfries	31,000	32,863
Stanford Hall, Leicestershire	25,320	31,382
Breamore House, Hampshire	26,332	27,885
Luton Hoo, Beds	32,159	27,637

Fritton listed as thirteenth most popular national tourist site in 1982

For a few years we had an American 8th Air Force museum in the barn. It later moved to Thorpe Abbott. We tried crafts, and basket-making proved the most popular. An information centre gave details of the lake in wartime when the amphibious tanks trained there. I was away at the time in the Western Desert, and so I missed Winston Churchill and General Montgomery sizing up training there before

Craft demonstrations proved popular attractions

D-Day. During my years at the lake several men who had trained or had been stationed in the area came to visit. A retired officer was brought along one day. Apparently, he lost many men in France after training at Fritton. He was pushed around the grounds in a wheelchair. It was his last request to return to the lake as it had played such an important role in his life. The lake has had that effect on many people – perhaps the invisible allure of Freya.

One man I'll always remember is Ron Mole. He trained at Fritton and told how a small number of tanks and men who started off were still there on VE Day. It was with great pride that he spoke of Fritton Lake.

A new road was put in – not before time – I can recall 17 coaches parked in one afternoon. A caravan park

opened for rallies and club sites. Home-made sausage
rolls and scones were favourites. Peggy would start
work at 7am or even earlier, boiling over 100 eggs for
sandwiches and also
sorting out ham, cheese
and fish. About 500 on a
busy day and half a
hundredweight of scones.
It's incredible what we eat!

In August 1984 over 62,000
visitors came, including a
certain person with the
idea of taking over when I
retired. She was good, but
put off by this experience. The poor girl was kept
very busy from the day she arrived until the day she
left. You might say she was put off for life. No
country parks for her after this lot!

Somerleyton staff
being presented to the
Queen by Lord
Somerleyton: Walter
Mussett stands in line
second from right

When life was truly hectic, Peggy and I were always
ready to set a good example, often taking over the
entrance till, shop and ice cream department until all
the others had finished lunch. We were lucky to have
a loyal team, and it was always easier to lead than to
drive. The weather played an important role, of
course, and I remember how snow one Easter
restricted numbers to about 100. We made up for that
later.

In 21 years at Fritton, 19 of them as manager and the
other two helping on days off and with literature
distribution, we met people from all walks of life.

Through the kindness of Lord Somerleyton I was introduced to Her Majesty the Queen, an experience

I shall never forget. There were happy events, many of them to raise funds for charities, including the popular plastic duck race. Sheila Chadwick and Doris Day were the two secretaries who put up with me. I thank them most sincerely for their help and patience. Like all the Lake staff, they got used to my ways.

A Wheelyboat, the Walter Mussett, *helps wheelchair visitors to explore the lake*

Dominating the scene at all times was that wonderful lake, a source of economic benefit but also the sort of natural facility that helped make so much hard work a pleasure. I never took it for granted, never tired of its charms and watched folk of all ages discover its secrets. The magic never faded – and it's still there whenever I go back.

I was lucky to have such a fine team of lads to look after our boats over the years. I recall one who saved a man who fell into the lake at the boathouse. A large man and a small boy: 'How did you manage to get him out?' I asked. 'I got under him and pushed his head up' said the lad. He later joined the Royal Navy. At first, it was rowing only for me to go out and control the boats. Then I was allowed to have an outboard engine, a great help. Red deer roamed the

83

woods around the lake. Lovely to see them, but they did some damage. Over the years efforts were made to reduce numbers of eels and pike in the lake. Now it seems nature can do it on its own. I once had the delight of a trip over Fritton in a Tiger Moth. My goodness, how different the lake and other amenities looked from above. Planning can be made easier and costly errors avoided.

We had only one fatal accident involving boats during my 21 years at Fritton. A full inquiry was carried out and safety procedures checked to see that all was in order. Much to my relief signs and warnings had been repainted only two weeks before

Where the formal gardens meet the lake – a favourite spot for visitors

A dinghy on the lake

the incident, and an adult was on duty on the lake when it happened. A group of boys hired a boat and went across the lake to Lord Somerleyton's boathouse to take out a canoe. News reached us that a boy was missing and the police were called. Divers came and a body was recovered from the lake only a few yards from the boathouse.

This was a rare cloud of concern over beautiful Fritton Lake, my permanent home for over two decades. Progress had exceeded our wildest expectations and I was proud to hand over the running of this venture in such fine shape. We had turned the place round, as they say, pushing

85

Happy landings on
the snake slide ...

attendances up from 100 a day to 5000-plus on Bank
Holidays. It provided me and my family with a good
living and all who came to see us were guaranteed a
good day out.

There could be no possible room for regrets over
taking that momentous decision to leave the world of
gamekeeping and go into the leisure industry. I
always listened to what the public wanted and also
tried to meet with what my employers deemed

*... happy anglers at
the lake's side*

necessary for a proper income. I was always ready to compromise in a bid to keep both of them satisfied as far as possible. I didn't spend money for the sake of it, but I recognised the need to keep up to date in an increasingly competitive field and, where possible, to stay one step ahead of other local attractions.

So it was with sadness and pride that in 1987 I took my last lingering look as 'master' of the lake and all the facilities surrounding it. I go back regularly. It's like calling on an old friend, a faithful old friend with whom I shared so many good times.

Walter and Peggy

Walter officially retired in 1987, but carried on helping out at Fritton for the next two years, mainly with the distribution of literature about the Country Park and standing in for the new manager on his days off. Not surprisingly, Walter found himself almost as busy in his retirement as he had been in his working life. To this day he remains keenly interested in the lake and the ongoing development of the business that he started .

The year before I retired Peggy and I moved from the main house to Frogs Hole Cottage at Herringfleet. We lived there for 12 years, and after that moved to Mundham. Until I turned 80, in 2002, I went back regularly to Morningthorpe to help out on shoot days. Now I just go over on odd days. Some guns who shot at Morningthorpe also shot at Somerleyton, so I kept in touch with a lot of people.

Pleasantly surprised by a strippagram girl

There was a big surprise when I was given the full 'This Is Your Life' treatment at my retirement party on 3rd October 1987. So many of my old friends were there – not to mention a strippagram girl! – and I was even presented with a 'big red book' with pictures, cartoons and tributes from many people including Lord and Lady Somerleyton. There was a message from all the Fritton staff, saying 'Fritton Lake will seem a strange place without you'. And Peggy and I would feel strange without Fritton Lake.

We planned to travel more when I retired, and had enough money to go to Australia and New Zealand, something we had always wanted to do. But somehow we didn't use it, and then we bought a motor home and travelled around in that for five years instead. All summer we would go away for two weeks, come home for two weeks and see to the garden, then go away for two weeks, and so on. We did the whole of the British Isles in that way.

I was interested to see some of the new attractions that opened at Fritton after my retirement. The nine-hole par three golf course and the 18-hole putting green remain big attractions, but nowadays there is also a family cycle trail and an orienteering course.

The heavy horse stables were opened in 1993, with working Shire horses and Suffolk Punches – the rarest of the heavy horse breeds. 1994 saw the birth of the first Shire horse on the Somerleyton Estate for more than 40 years: it was named Fritton Lake Jester.

Another major venture after I left was the falconry centre, which also opened in 1993. It is home to a varied collection of birds of prey from different families and habitats around the world, many of which can be seen flying free during daily demonstrations.

The adventure playground which my sons helped to build has changed, but it's still there and still popular. Some things have gone, including the giant mushrooms that were so popular with the young children but others have been added, like giant outdoor board games.

The latest development at Fritton is, you might say, an extension of the holiday cottage business which Peggy and I started all those years ago. Fritton Lake Woodland Lodges is a new holiday home development on the shores of the lake, where people can buy their own timber-built holiday home. In the busy world we live in today, I think families appreciate the tranquillity and seclusion of the lake more than ever.

My first visit to a duck decoy was in 1937, the summer after I left school at the age of 14. Little did I imagine that more than 60 years later I would be advising on the construction of a new decoy at Fritton Lake.

In 1999 the present manager of Fritton Lake, Edward Knowles, approached the Great Yarmouth Wildfowlers and Conservation Association with the idea of restoring a decoy pipe where it would be accessible for the public visiting Fritton Lake Countryworld. He wanted to allow visitors to see more of the lake as it used to be, and to appreciate old country skills that are now all but lost. I was asked to advise on the design and siting of the decoy. A band of volunteers helped with the work through the summer of 1999 and 2000 reshaping the ditch, making the hoops and putting them in position. In 2001 the reed screens and netting were added to complete the project. After a few hiccups, the new decoy, which is situated in Church Bay, is due to open to the public this year [2003].

Fritton is a magical place. I never grow tired of it.

Walter Mussett and the
sporting author
J. Wentworth Day in 1954

I was raised in rural Norfolk at a time when genuine countryside characters abounded. A walk down the village street or across the nearest pastures invariably led to meetings with familiar figures ready to share their time of day. Quiet wisdom, gentle humour and a deep sense of satisfaction at simply being there were the trademarks on parade. The highest accolade for anyone displaying them was to be dubbed 'a good old boy'.

This heartfelt description came out of semi-retirement when I chatted to Walter Mussett's family and friends about his countryman qualities. Affection and admiration flowed easily towards that delightfully old-fashioned label. 'He's a good old boy' may echo gentler, slower, more parochial days but Walter's home-made virtues would shine across the headlands of any era.

At ease with people of all classes, and of contrasting means, he eagerly embraced the 'hard-work' ethic throughout his life on land and lake. It was nothing unusual for him to be gainfully employed from 4.30am through to midnight. And he expected the same sort of solid graft and dedication from those around him. He pays generous tribute to his 'top team', wife Peggy and sons John and Gordon, and it is clear how their support and shared enthusiasms helped to write fresh chapters in the Fritton Lake success story.

Walter's dramatic switch from gamekeeping to a key role in the burgeoning local leisure industry underlines a flair for adaptability unknown to the vast majority of countryfolk – even in these diversification-led times. Yes, he was returning to familiar territory, but it was still a mighty big gamble to leave a scene he knew so well and back his own judgment as a potential businessman alongside the likes of Lord Somerleyton and other big noises in the tourist trade.

That he took such a gamble in the first place says a lot about Walter's self-confidence. That he made a resounding success of it says plenty more about the steely character beneath the avuncular smile.

Walter lives in well-earned retirement with Peggy at Mundham, where his garden flourishes and fond memories blossom. He carries the air of a well-contented man able to reflect on jobs well done. Far-flung travels in recent years include visits to Portugal, Canada, South Africa, the Mediterranean and USA. 'All very nice,' muses Walter, 'but I'm just as happy wandering quietly round Fritton Lake. It's a beautiful spot…'

A good old boy shields his eyes as he peers over glistening waters. The action turns, almost imperceptibly, into a personal salute to the lovely lake which first captivated him nearly 70 years ago.

POSTSCRIPT

Walter Mussett

I am very fortunate in having had the opportunity to work with, or be of service to, people from all walks of life. Some of them are real 'characters' and not easily forgotten.

One such character who became a good friend was Arthur Pearson. He and his wife lived next door to my family when we moved to Somerleyton Laurel Loke in 1934. Lady Bridget later renamed it Floral Loke after we had tidied up the gardens and put in the flower beds. Arthur – or 'Lugs' as he was affectionately known on account of his big ears – had been coachman to one of the previous estate agents, Kerry Rix, and his knowledge of the estate was greatly valued by Lord and Lady Somerleyton and the then estate agent, Captain Flatt. He was a kind and helpful person, a keen football supporter who took me by train to see Norwich City play their first match at Carrow Road after they had moved there from the Nest in 1935.

I wish particularly to thank the Crossley (Somerleyton) family. After I left Somerleyton school I began my working life with them, and it was thanks to the present Lord and Lady Somerleyton's father and mother that I became a gamekeeper. I am also grateful to the present Lord and Lady Somerleyton for allowing me to take my chance at Fritton, and make it work.

I would also like to thank Mr and Mrs Hugh Sargent for their kindness in inviting me to Morningthorpe, where we as a family enjoyed our nine-year stay. My thanks also to the rest of the Sargent family and guns – I appreciate being invited back there on shooting days.

The workers at the Somerleyton and Morningthorpe estates are too numerous to name individually, but I would like to thank them all. Your efforts were appreciated.

Peggy and I spent some most enjoyable breaks in Hampshire with Harold and Gloria and family, and with Winnie and Sidney and their family in Leicestershire. Our sincere thanks to them all.

And last, but most important, I wish to thank my dear wife Peggy and our sons John and Gordon. You helped so much and without you my achievements would be so small.

Picture credits

The Tagman Press wishes to thank in particular Fritton Lake Countryworld, Lord Somerleyton, the Sargent family of Morningthorpe Manor and the Mussett family for their kind permission to reproduce photographs they have provided and in which they hold the copyright. Grateful thanks are also due to the following for their permission to reproduce other photographs: East Anglian Daily Times, *the* Great Yarmouth Mercury, *Peter Calvert of Lowestoft, the Camera Shop, Norwich, the Great Yarmouth News Agency, Studio 161 Lowestoft, Sawyer & Bird of Norwich, Coe Photographers, Norwich, Richard Tilbrook, and H Jenkins Ltd of Lowestoft. Every effort has been made to trace the copyright holders of other material.*